INVESTING FOR KIDS ACTIVITY BOOK

INVESTING
for Kids
ACTIVITY BOOK

65 Activities about Saving, Investing, and Growing Your Money

Justine Nelson

CALLISTO PUBLISHING

To my daughter, Quinn. May you find a bright
financial future in whatever you do.

Published by Callisto Publishing LLC C/O Sourcebooks LLC
P.O. Box 4410, Naperville, Illinois 60567-4410
(630) 961-3900
callistopublishing.com

This product conforms to all applicable CPSC and CPSIA standards.

Source of Production: 1010 Printing Asia Limited, Kwun Tong, Hong Kong, China
Date of Production: August 2023
Run Number: SBCAL123

Printed and bound in China.
1010 9

Contents

All about Investing **1**

SAVING AND GROWING MONEY

INVESTING MONEY

All about Investing

As a twelve-year-old, I knew how to earn money through babysitting, but I didn't really know what to do with the money I earned. I decided to blow most of it at the mall on clothes or chocolate chip cookies! It wasn't until after I graduated from college and paid off $35,000 in student loan debt that I realized there are better ways to use money. I could save for things I wanted and make my money grow by investing in the stock market.

Investing money can allow you to quit your job early, give to others, and buy things that matter most to you. Money is a tool. You can either build something amazing with it or make a mess of things. This activity book will help you use money to your benefit.

Inside, you'll find activities focused on the following: *Making Money, Responsible Spending, Saving and Growing Money,* and *Investing Money*. You'll learn what a rate of return is, how to develop a business idea, and how to save and spend money on things that you love! This book is designed to be done in order, so start with *Making Money* first.

By the way, you won't need any actual money or investments to do these activities. All you'll need is a pencil and an adult's help to go on the internet when instructed. Remember, you shouldn't (and won't be able to) open accounts or invest money without an adult's approval and assistance.

Imagine being able to understand how to invest and grow your money. You could even become the money expert among your friends and family! Ready to get started? See you inside!

Justine Nelson

MONEY IS EVERYWHERE

Look around your home or neighborhood. Can you think of ways to earn money? A bowl of lemons can be turned into lemonade that you can sell. A neighbor might need help watering their plants. Write down all of your ideas. A list is a useful tool that can help you get started quickly.

Review the list below. Put a check mark next to each thing you can do now to earn money. Stick to activities that sound like fun. You are more likely to stay with a job when you are having fun! Use the blank lines to fill in new ideas of your own. Then count how many ways you can earn money. Ask permission from a parent or guardian before you get started with each activity.

☐ Babysit siblings or neighborhood kids

☐ Wash cars

☐ Help an elderly person with chores or taking care of their pets

☐ Sell lemonade

☐ Take photos for others

☐ Start a dog-walking service

☐ Offer pet-grooming services

☐ Sell unwanted toys or clothes

☐ Sell baked goods

☐ Sell homemade crafts

☐ Water plants

☐ Start a lawn care business

☐ House-sit for neighbors

☐ Shovel driveways

☐ Become a tutor to other kids

☐ Collect mail for neighbors while they're away

☐ Help with odd jobs and errands

☐ _____

☐ _____

CASH-MAKING CAREERS

Do you know what you want to be when you grow up? There are endless ways to do something you love and earn money at the same time. However, not all jobs make the same amount of money.

A salary is money that is paid to someone for their work. Salaries are usually listed as annual income—the total amount of money you'd be paid in one year. In the table below, write down three jobs that sound interesting to you. Then, with an adult's help, research the salary of each job and record it below.

JOB THAT I WANT TO DO WHEN I GET OLDER	SALARY
1.	
2.	
3.	

Which job has the highest salary? _____

Which job are you most excited to explore? _____

Talk to an adult about what you would do each day in that job and how much money you could earn.

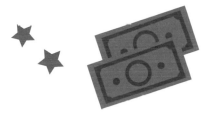

HOW DO YOU VIEW MONEY?

Do you believe money is bad? Do you believe more money makes you happier? Doctors Brad and Ted Klontz found that most people have one of four major money beliefs:

Money Avoider: I avoid money because I believe money is bad. Money also makes me anxious.

Money Worshipper: I believe more money creates more happiness.

Money Status: I believe how much money I have determines how I feel about myself.

Money Vigilant: I believe money should be saved. I don't talk about money and keep that information private.

Let's see how you view money! For each scenario below, circle the letter next to the statement that best describes you. Which letter did you circle most? Find the money belief matching that letter on the following page.

1. **When I hold a dollar bill in my hands, I feel . . .**
    A. I don't deserve to have this dollar.
    B. I need more than one dollar bill.
    C. I could use it to make my life better.
    D. I should save it in case I need it later.

2. **When something is broken, I want to . . .**
    A. ignore it.
    B. earn money to replace it.
    C. trash it.
    D. fix it myself.

3. **If I had more money, I would . . .**
   A. give away what I don't need.
   B. have fewer problems.
   C. feel better about life.
   D. save it.

4. **Someone who doesn't have a lot of money . . .**
   A. is still a good person and doesn't need more money.
   B. is not happy.
   C. is lazy.
   D. should work harder to be able to save more money.

Mostly As: Money Avoider

Mostly Bs: Money Worshipper

Mostly Cs: Money Status

Mostly Ds: Money Vigilant

MOWING FOR MONEY

A job can help you earn money to save, spend, give, or invest. It's important to look for work opportunities that also fit your schedule. Most kids aren't able to work during school hours, so they have to get creative about how to use their time after school or on the weekends to earn money. Read the following problem and answer the questions below. Then check your answers in the answer key.

Megan wants to earn $100 per week by mowing lawns in her neighborhood. She has five hours of free time each week to mow lawns. She knows that it takes her one hour to mow each lawn. Megan wants to figure out how much to charge for each lawn so that she can make the most of her time.

1. How many lawns can Megan mow in a week? _____

2. How much should she charge per lawn? _____

MONEY-MOTIVATED

Money is a tool that can help you throughout your life, but you might need some motivation to help you earn it. Whether you want to use money to go to college or buy a new pair of shoes, it is helpful to have reasons to earn money. Check off the reasons below that you have for earning money. Use the blank lines to fill in reasons of your own. Then circle your top three reasons. Talk to an adult about why you chose your top three reasons.

☐ Buy new clothes

☐ Invest in the stock market

☐ Give to friends or family

☐ Buy new toys or games

☐ Give to charity

☐ Buy gifts for others

☐ Go to a concert

☐ Buy souvenirs on vacation

☐ Buy a scooter

☐ Buy school supplies

☐ Feel independent

☐ Go to a restaurant

☐ Go to college

☐ Pay for food

☐ _____

☐ _____

☐ _____

☐ _____

WHAT KIND OF WORKER ARE YOU?

Do you like to come up with ideas and let others carry out your plan? Or would you rather work on an activity that someone else assigns to you? You can earn money as a leader or a team player, but knowing how you work best can help you find a job that you'll enjoy.

Let's see what type of worker you are! For each scenario below, circle the letter next to the response that best describes you. Which letter did you circle most? Find the worker type with that letter on the following page.

1. If I worked at a pizza shop, I would like to . . .
   A. be the delivery driver.
   B. make sure the staff makes the pizzas on time.
   C. come up with a plan to sell more pizzas.

2. When I play a game, I like to . . .
   A. follow the rules.
   B. make sure everyone else is following the rules.
   C. make up the rules.

3. When I'm at recess, I like to . . .
   A. stick to the swing set.
   B. be team captain for dodgeball.
   C. come up with a new game and have everyone play.

Mostly As: Team Player

You are great at following instructions and enjoy doing tasks on your own. Software engineers and X-ray technicians are good examples of team players.

Mostly Bs: Leader

You like to guide others and make decisions to help everyone be successful. Coaches and business managers are great leaders.

Mostly Cs: CEO

You like creating new ideas and enjoy trying new things. Entrepreneurs and engineers make great CEOs.

JOB SCOUTING

There are thousands of jobs in the world. From designing skyscrapers as an architect to coding software as a computer programmer, the possibilities are endless. A great way to learn more about jobs is to ask the people who already do them.

Think about an adult you know who has a job. They could be a person working at the library, a family member, or your teacher. Ask them these questions about their job and record their answers below.

What activities do you do each day as part of your job? _____

_____

What is the best part of your job? _____

If someone wants to do the same job as you when they're older,

what advice would you give them? _____

_____

What type of education do you need to do your job? _____

_____

Now write down your thoughts about this job. Is it something you

would like to do? _____

_____

CURRENCY CONVERSIONS

Different countries use different forms of currency. The United States uses American dollars, China uses the yuan; France uses the euro; and Brazil uses the real. When you visit another country, you can exchange, or trade, American dollars for that country's currency.

When currency is converted, it goes through an exchange rate. An exchange rate is the value of one currency versus another. The exchange rate changes depending on the global market. Some days, the American dollar will have more value than the Chinese yuan. Other days, the dollar will be worth less. With help from an adult, research three different currencies and fill in the table. You can use the examples on this page, or look up currencies for other countries you'd like to visit someday.

TYPE OF FOREIGN CURRENCY	ONE AMERICAN DOLLAR IS WORTH

TAX TIME

When you earn a paycheck from your job, taxes will be taken out of your paycheck. For example, you may earn $1,000, but you will take home less because the government takes some money as taxes.

The government uses money from taxes to help the community. Federal tax is collected by the federal government to pay for the country's roads, improve education, or provide disaster relief. A state tax is used to pay for similar things, but just for that state. The taxes you pay depend on how much you make and your tax rate. Use the information below to figure out the taxes you'd have to pay on $1,000. Then check your answers in the answer key.

Paycheck = $1,000

Federal tax rate = 10%

State tax rate = 5%

1. How much federal tax do you have to pay? _____

2. How much state tax do you have to pay? _____

3. How much money do you take home after you

pay taxes? _____

PAYMENT AND CASH CATEGORIES

There are many ways to pay for things. Paper bills and coins have been around for hundreds of years, but today we can use things like credit and b cards or mobile apps to pay for goods and services. Credit cards and apps by themselves are not money. They are a form of payment people can use to purchase things without using physical money like bills and coins.

Do you know the difference between types of money and types of payment? Look at the following list and put each item in the correct column. Check the answer key to see if you got it right!

- **$10 bill**
- **check**
- **credit card**
- **$1 bill**
- **quarter**
- **money order**
- **dime**
- **app (like Venmo or Google Pay)**
- **debit card**
- **$20 bill**

TYPES OF MONEY	TYPES OF PAYMENT

BUILD A BUSINESS BLUEPRINT

Building a business lets you dream of new solutions to everyday problems. It also means you will be your own boss! Anyone can start a business, but a smart business owner creates a business plan, or blueprint, before they get started.

A business plan usually includes these things:

Mission statement: one sentence that explains the business and its goals.

Products and services: what you are selling—either a product (like cookies) or a service (such as washing cars). Include your pricing and how your business can help customers.

Market research: an investigation into businesses like yours and your customers. Who is your competition? Do customers want what you are selling? It's good to ask people you know if your product or service is something they would buy.

Marketing: a plan for how you will get customers. This could include passing out flyers around your neighborhood or getting help from an adult to post your business online. Get creative!

Expenses: a list of things you need to pay for to start and run your business. For example, you would need to buy soap for a car wash business.

It's time to build your own business plan! Fill in the following sections to create your first business plan. Then use the plan as a guide to start your business.

I want to sell a (circle one):   product   service

My one-sentence mission statement: _____

Products and services: _____

DESCRIPTION	PRICE	HOW DOES IT HELP PEOPLE?

Market research: _____

_____

_____

_____

Marketing: _____

_____

_____

_____

Expenses: _____   _____

_____   _____

_____   _____

THAT'S HOW THE COOKIE CRUMBLES

Imagine selling delicious cookies to your friends and family. They get a sweet treat and you make money. It's a win-win! However, you will need to buy ingredients to make the cookies and bags to put the cookies in. These costs are called "business expenses"—the money it takes to run your business.

In order to make a profit (money earned minus the amount of money spent) you need to know how much each cookie costs to make. Use the information below to answer the questions, then check your work in the answer key.

Business expenses = *Total cost of running a business*
Profit = *Money earned – Business expenses*

Ingredients: $10
Bags: $5
Sign: $5
Number of cookies you can make: 50

1. What are the total business expenses?

_____

2. How much does each cookie cost to make?

_____

3. If you sold each cookie for $1, what is your profit?

_____

THE FOLLOW-THROUGH

Starting a job can be exciting! But after a while, a job can start to feel a little boring, or even get in the way of fun activities you want to do. It's important to stay motivated and keep your commitment to follow through.

When you follow through on a job, you earn a good reputation that can help you get another job or earn more money. When a job starts to feel like a chore, reread this page so you can reenergize yourself to stay committed.

State your why

   I want this job because: _____

Set a goal

   I want to earn money with this job so I can:

   _____

Have a backup plan

   If I can't complete my job, who could be a substitute for me?

   _____

Set priorities

   I would be okay skipping these activities for my job:

   _____

   The one activity that I don't want to skip for my job is:

   _____

RÉSUMÉ BUILDER

A résumé is a document that lists your work experience, skills, and reasons you would be a good fit for a job. Although many jobs for kids don't require a résumé, it's good practice to write one. Plus, many adults will pay attention to the thoughtfulness you put into applying for the job.

Résumés are usually made of these parts:

Summary: a one-sentence statement about what makes you the right person for the job. (Example: *Outdoorsy sixth grader looking to get mowing experience in local neighborhood.*)

List of relevant skills: skills you have that relate to the job. If you want to babysit, you could list skills like changing diapers or feeding toddlers.

Work experience: jobs you've had before that will help you with the new job. If you have never worked before, list experience from other activities such as student council or sports.

Use the template below to build your first résumé. Don't forget, ordinary chores like cleaning your room or taking out the trash count as experience! With your guardian's permission, you can hand in your résumé when you want to start a new job.

My name is: _____

Summary: _____

_____

These are the skills that I am good at: _____

_____

_____

My work experience includes: _____

_____

_____

I like to work (circle all that apply):

alone   with a partner   with a group

I am available to work these days and times:

	AVAILABLE	TIME (CIRCLE AM/PM)	
MONDAY	☐	____:____ AM / PM to	____:____ AM / PM
TUESDAY	☐	____:____ AM / PM to	____:____ AM / PM
WEDNESDAY	☐	____:____ AM / PM to	____:____ AM / PM
THURSDAY	☐	____:____ AM / PM to	____:____ AM / PM
FRIDAY	☐	____:____ AM / PM to	____:____ AM / PM
SATURDAY	☐	____:____ AM / PM to	____:____ AM / PM
SUNDAY	☐	____:____ AM / PM to	____:____ AM / PM

HOW TO MAKE WORK FUN

Getting paid for a job well done feels satisfying. It's even more satisfying when you make work fun. Think about chores or tasks that you do every day. Is it more fun to brush your teeth while listening to music? Does cleaning your room go faster when you can do it with a sibling or friend?

You can also mix fun activities into your job. When you have fun while you work, you get more done and are more positive! Put a check mark next to each activity that you think would make work more enjoyable. There are a few spaces to fill in ideas of your own. Discuss your choices with a guardian.

☐ Listen to music

☐ Wear a work uniform

☐ Track days worked with a sticker chart

☐ Work with a friend

☐ Have a set start and stop time

☐ Set a timer to see how fast and accurately you can work

☐ Create a work schedule

☐ Have a snack before you work

☐ Work with a sibling

☐ _____

☐ _____

☐ _____

PRICE CHECK PARTY

Shopping can be fun, but not when you pay more than you need to for something you want! A toy or game that is sold at one store may not be the same price at another store. That's why it's important to check the price at a few different stores to get the best deal.

Have an adult help you research the price of an item you wish to purchase. Check the cost of that item at four stores—either online or in person. Then record the price at each location below. Next, see if you can find any discounts or coupons that could lower the cost even more. Record those in the correct column. Which store has the best deal?

The item that I wish to purchase is a: _____

STORE OR WEBSITE	PRICE	DISCOUNT OR COUPON AVAILABLE?	FINAL PRICE

The store with the best deal is: _____

EXPENSE EXPLORER

Fixed expenses are things you need to pay for every month. Groceries are a fixed expense because we need to eat. Other things—like electricity, water, or paying to live in our homes—are also fixed expenses. A variable expense is something that may change from time to time. For example, you probably don't need to buy school supplies every month.

Knowing the difference between fixed and variable expenses can help you focus your spending on things you need versus things you want. As you get older, you'll have several expenses to pay, and you might need to choose which ones take priority. Be an expense explorer by grouping the following expenses under the correct expense column. Check the categories in the answer key.

- lunch money
- groceries
- phone app
- jeans
- pencils
- electricity
- movie tickets
- beach vacation
- transportation

FIXED EXPENSES	VARIABLE EXPENSES

FUN AND FREE

Many people think spending money brings happiness. Have you ever bought a piece of candy and felt happy about it? After you ate the candy, though, you might have felt like you needed to spend more money in order to feel happy again.

Happiness comes from fun experiences that don't always cost money. Think of things you like to do that are free and make you happy. It could be drawing, playing catch, or visiting a local park. In the spaces below, write all the ways you like to have fun that are also free to do. Then circle your three favorite activities. Be sure to mix these activities into your life so you can remind yourself that happiness is fun and free!

Fun and free activities I love to do:

_____   _____   _____

_____   _____   _____

_____   _____   _____

_____   _____   _____

_____   _____   _____

_____   _____   _____

_____   _____   _____

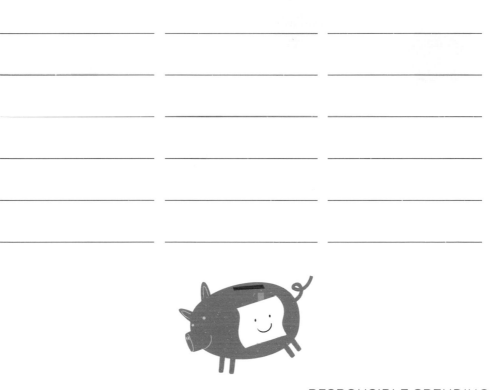

BUDGET-BUSTER

A budget is a written plan to track income and expenses. Budgets help people save money and spend it wisely. They are usually created every month. Without a monthly budget, people can't easily see how much they spend and might spend more money than they make. This can cause a lot of financial problems. A common way to keep spending under control is to use a zero-based budget.

A zero-based budget assigns every dollar of income to an expense or savings goal. The idea is that your income minus expenses and savings equals zero at the end of the month. A negative amount would mean that you are over budget and spending too much money. A positive amount means you are under budget. You can put any leftover money toward savings goals or spend it on something fun. That's the great thing about budgeting—you get to decide what to do with your money when you spend responsibly.

Now that you know how a zero-based budget works, it's time to look for some budget-busters. Malik recently started a budget to track his monthly income and expenses. Look at his budget on the following page and figure out which expenses could be reduced or eliminated so that Malik stays within budget. Then check the answer key to see how you did.

INCOME
$2,000

EXPENSES	AMOUNT
Rent	$700
Groceries	$300
Bills	$250
Gas	$100
Clothing	$125
Concerts	$350
Vacation fund	$100
Retirement	$150
Amount left:	

1. How much money is left over?

_____

2. Is Malik over or under budget?

_____

3. Which expenses could Malik eliminate or reduce so he stays within budget?

_____

WHAT KIND OF BUDGETER ARE YOU?

You can create a budget as soon as you start earning money—but budgets are not one-size-fits-all. Some methods are best for those who like to write things down. Others are good for those who prefer using a computer or website. You can choose spreadsheets, notebooks, or a budgeting app.

If you pick the best method for you, it will be easier for you to budget regularly. Take the quiz below to figure out which budgeting method is right for you. For each of the scenarios, circle the letter next to the response that best describes you. Which letter did you circle most? Find the budget method with that letter on the following page.

1. **When I want to remember something, I . . .**
   A. add it to a calendar.
   B. write it down.
   C. use an app to set a reminder.

2. **When I work on a math problem, I . . .**
   A. write down the easy stuff and use a calculator for the hard stuff.
   B. write it down on a sheet of paper.
   C. use a calculator as much as I can.

3. **When I'm doing a classroom activity, I love using a . . .**
   A. notebook and the computer.
   B. notebook.
   C. computer program.

Mostly As: Digital-Doer

Digital spreadsheets are for you! Spreadsheets need some hands-on work, but you can easily add formulas to do the math for you.

Mostly Bs: Notetaker

You'll do great with a dedicated financial notebook—or even a whiteboard—to help you stay on track.

Mostly Cs: App Enthusiast

Your budgeting brain works best with an app. You'll enjoy seeing how easy it is to set up and check your budget on the go.

DEBT IS DANGEROUS

Debt, or a loan, is borrowed money (usually from a bank) that you have to pay back. You must repay most debt with interest on a schedule. Interest is additional money you pay for borrowing money. Debt wouldn't be so bad if interest rates weren't high, but the longer it takes to pay back a debt, the more money you'll owe. People go into debt for all sorts of things:

- buying a car
- buying a house
- starting a business
- going to college
- personal spending

If you don't pay back your debts on time, moneylenders could sue you or garnish your wages—that means they can take money from your paycheck. With an adult's help, go online and look up the average debt owed for each item listed below.

Car loan: _____

Home loan: _____

Business loan: _____

Student loan: _____

MONEY MANAGEMENT

What do you do with your money once you earn it? Do you immediately spend it or hold on to it? A great money manager can do both!
You can put your money into three major money buckets.

Spend: You can use the money immediately on whatever you want (within reason and with permission from a guardian).

Save: You can use the money for things you are saving for, like a tablet computer.

Give: You can give the money to people who need it—a charity, church, or even a friend.

Are you a responsible money manager? Think about ways you can spend, save, or give. Write down your ideas under each money bucket. Then talk to an adult about how you can complete one idea from each category.

SPEND	SAVE	GIVE
_____	_____	_____
_____	_____	_____
_____	_____	_____
_____	_____	_____
_____	_____	_____

CREATING A CREDIT SCORE

A credit score is a measurement of how well you handle debt. It tells lenders how responsible you are as a spender and how likely you are to pay back your debts on time. Those who pay their bills on time—like credit cards or electricity bills—and have been doing so for a long time earn a good credit score. A good credit score can help you get approval for loans or credit cards. It can even help you get a good deal on car insurance and renting an apartment later in life.

Credit scores can range from 300 to 850. The higher your credit score is, the more opportunities you will have financially. A low credit score can hurt your chances of buying a home or applying for things like credit cards.

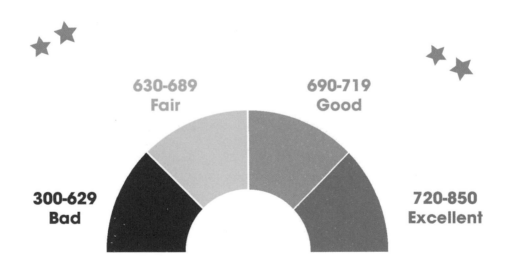

So, how do you make sure you have an excellent credit score? Start by being a responsible spender! Below is a list of activities that can affect your credit score. Check the boxes of activities that you think would *improve* a credit score. Then check the answer key on page 85 and make these healthy financial habits part of your life.

☐ Paying bills on time

☐ Ignoring debt that you owe

☐ Paying the electric bill each month

☐ Spending money on things you can afford

☐ Paying your credit card bill each month

☐ Not paying off a car loan

☐ Paying off student loans

☐ Skipping a loan payment that you owe

☐ Adding more debt on a credit card that you can't pay back

INTEREST IN ACTION

If your credit card isn't paid by the end of the month, interest gets added to what you owe. Then interest is charged the following month on your new total owed. It is a tough cycle to break! Credit card interest is usually listed as an annual percentage rate, or APR. Even though it's an annual (yearly) rate, credit card companies charge interest based on what you owe each month.

In order to calculate how much interest you are being charged, you will need to know three things: the APR, credit card balance, and number of days in your billing statement.

APR ÷ 365 (number of days in the year) = Daily rate

Daily rate × Credit card balance = Daily interest charge

Daily interest charge × 30 days (number of days in a billing cycle) = Total interest charged for the month

Imagine you bought $500 worth of games and clothes on a credit card and didn't pay it off. If there are thirty days in your billing cycle, calculate the total interest charged for the month using the different APRs below. Then check the answer key and see how you did.

1. What is your monthly interest if your credit card APR is 15% (0.15)?

_____

2. What is your monthly interest if your credit card APR is 22% (0.22)?

_____

3. What is your monthly interest if your credit card APR is 30% (0.30)?

_____

SPOT THE SALE

Paying full price for things can quickly drain any money you earned from a job. Smart shoppers compare costs of similar items so they can get a good deal and keep more money in their wallets. A pair of jeans might cost $50 at full price, but take a look at the sales or clearance rack and you could see a similar pair for half price!

Can you spot any sales? Get permission from an adult to go online or into a store to look for items on sale. Then compare a similar item that isn't on sale. Record the cost difference for each item below and decide which feels better to purchase.

ITEM	COST OF SALE ITEM	COST OF REGULAR PRICED ITEM	COST DIFFERENCE

DEBIT VS. CREDIT

When you open a bank account, you might hear the terms debit and credit. But what do these words mean?

Debit: money that goes *out* of the account.

Credit: money that comes *into* the account.

Credits include things like your income, dividends, or interest paid to your account by the bank. Dividends are profits a company gives to its shareholders (people who have stock or shares in a company). Debits are any expenses, such as paying for groceries or a new bicycle. Figure out if the items below are debits or credits, then check your answers in the answer key.

Yuki just opened a bank account and has a few credits and debits that need to be organized. She earned a paycheck and some interest on the account. Yuki also bought groceries, ordered a new computer, and paid her electricity bill.

Which items belong in the debit category? _____

_____

Which items belong in the credit category? _____

_____

THE SAVINGS EQUATION

Have you ever wanted to buy something but felt discouraged because it was too expensive? Adults can feel the same way. Instead of being patient and saving for a big item, some adults borrow money by using a credit card and don't pay it back on time. As a result, they go into debt and get charged interest. It's not a good habit to start!

Use a simple equation to help you save for your goals. The idea is to break down the cost into monthly payments to yourself. Then you can put the monthly payments into a savings account or in a safe place at home. There are two ways to use the savings equation:

Total cost ÷ How much you can save each month
= Number of months to complete goal

Total cost ÷ Number of months to complete goal
= How much you need to save each month

Let's say you want to buy a new art supply set that costs $30, but you can save only $10 per month. That means in three months you will be able to buy the art supply set ($30 ÷ $10 = 3). Fill in the table below to figure out how much you need to save each month for each item or when you can complete each savings goal. Check your answers in the answer key.

SAVINGS GOAL	TOTAL COST	MONTHLY SAVINGS AMOUNT	NUMBER OF MONTHS TO COMPLETE GOAL
VIDEO GAME CONSOLE	$400	$50	
TICKET TO DISNEY WORLD	$150		12
ART SUPPLY SET	$50	$25	
HEADPHONES	$80		2

OUT OF HABIT

Many people spend money out of habit. Some people spend money because they want something new, whereas others save what they have. Your spending habits can be shaped by how you see adults or friends spend money. It's important to look at your own spending habits so that you can be more mindful of how you manage money.

Check the box next to each statement that is true about you. Then circle the statement that is the most important to you right now.

☐ I like to buy candy in the grocery store checkout.

☐ I think a long time about a purchase before I buy it.

☐ If my best friend has a new game, I want it, too.

☐ I talk to my parents or guardian about things I want to buy.

☐ I buy school lunch without looking at the cost.

☐ I look at the price tag when I want to buy something.

☐ I like to spend money as soon as I earn it.

☐ I like to hold on to money to save up for something big.

☐ I don't mind spending my own money on someone else.

☐ It feels good to give my money to charity.

DIRECT YOUR DOLLARS

You might think that a budget keeps you from spending, but it's actually the opposite. It gives you permission to spend on the things that matter most to you while decreasing your spending on things that don't. When you start earning money, a budget is a great way to direct your dollars.

It's wise to budget for things you wish to purchase. Select four items that you want to save money for. Then, go back to *The Savings Equation* activity on page 35 to calculate how much money you should budget for each item, and fill out the table below. There are a few ideas listed here, but feel free to come up with goals of your own!

- game
- backpack
- vacation souvenirs
- shoes
- candy

- theme park tickets
- sports game tickets
- scooter or bike
- book

ITEM	TOTAL COST	MONTHLY SAVINGS AMOUNT	NUMBER OF MONTHS TO COMPLETE GOAL

WHAT'S YOUR SPENDER TYPE?

Some kids are natural spenders, while others rarely spend money. It's the same way with adults. When you understand what type of spender you are, it can help you manage your money as you get older. Spending money is not wrong. Just be careful about how often you spend and on what types of items.

What's your spender type? For each scenario below, circle the letter next to the response that best describes you. Which letter did you circle most? Find the spender type with that letter on the following page.

1. **When I go into a store, I . . .**
   A. immediately find something to buy.
   B. take my time browsing.
   C. look around, but I don't buy anything.

2. **When I want a new game, I . . .**
   A. don't want to wait, because I need it now.
   B. look for discounts or coupons.
   C. ask my friends if they have it so I can use it.

3. **When I think about how I spent money last month, I . . .**
   A. spent money every week.
   B. spent money, but not often.
   C. didn't spend money.

Mostly As: Natural Spender

You like to spend money and do it often. Be careful to spend on things that matter to you.

Mostly Bs: Careful Spender

You like to spend money only after thinking about all of your options. You don't mind waiting for a sale in order to get a good deal.

Mostly Cs: Rare Spender

You don't spend money often. You'd rather save money until you really need to use it.

NOW OR LATER?

Nicholas Now and Lucy Later each earn $5 per week. They want to buy a new game that costs $20, but they also want to buy candy. Nicholas spends all of his money on candy for two weeks and saves nothing. Lucy decides to spend only $1 on candy and save $4 every week for the game. Starting in week three, Nicholas decides to save $5 and doesn't buy any more candy.

Fill in the table to show how much money Nicholas Now and Lucy Later save and spend each week. Then figure out how many weeks it will take each of them to save enough money to buy the game. Check the answer key to see if you got it right.

WEEKS	NICHOLAS NOW		LUCY LATER	
	SPENT	TOTAL SAVED	SPENT	TOTAL SAVED
WEEK 1	$5	$0	$1	$4
WEEK 2	$5	$0	$1	$8
WEEK 3				
WEEK 4				
WEEK 5				
WEEK 6				

SAVING AND GROWING MONEY

SIMPLE CENTS

Someone who borrows money is usually charged simple interest—the amount of money charged on a loan. For example, when you borrow money to pay for a car, you are usually charged simple interest. When you pay back your loan, you also need to pay the interest. Use this equation to answer the questions below, then check your responses in the answer key.

> **Simple interest = P × i × n**
>
> **P = Principal** (the amount you borrowed)
>
> **i = Interest rate**
>
> **n = Term** (how many years it takes to pay back the loan)

Sam decides to borrow money to pay for a car. He takes out a car loan for $25,000 (the principal). If the interest rate is 4% (or 0.04), how much interest will he have to pay over three years?

_____   _____

How much does Sam need to pay to completely pay off his

car loan? _____

GOAL-GETTER

There are two types of savings goals: short-term and long-term. Short-term savings goals are things you can save for in a few weeks, such as a treat from the grocery store. Long-term savings goals could take several months to complete, such as saving for a new bike. Expensive things take longer to save for since you need more time to earn and save money.

Can you spot the difference between short-term and long-term savings goals? Draw a star next to each item that is a long-term savings goal. Then, circle any items that are short-term savings goals. Hint: Items that are less expensive are usually short-term savings goals. Research the cost if you're unsure, then check your answers in the answer key.

- candy
- colored pencil set
- sneakers
- headphones
- video game console

- board game
- book
- puzzle
- phone
- basketball

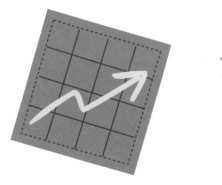

COMPOUND INTEREST

Compound interest is a great way to grow your money. Compound interest is interest that is paid to you based on the money you start with (the principal), plus all the interest you've earned on that money in the past. This is how many savings accounts work. Money in stock investments and index funds grows in a similar way through compound growth.

You can figure out the total investment amount with compound interest using this equation:

$P \times (1 + i)^n$

P = Principal (the money you start with)

i = Interest rate

n = Term (how many years you're saving)

1 = Principal plus interest (If your interest rate is 0.03, then the principal plus interest is 1.03.)

Use this equation to solve the following problem. You can also use an online interest calculator if you need help with the math. There is one in the Resources section on page 88. Check the answer key when you're finished.

Carmen wants to invest $5,000 in a savings account. If the interest rate for the account is 3% (or 0.03), what will her money be worth in 25 years?

SIMPLE VS. COMPOUND INTEREST

When you compare simple and compound interest side by side, there doesn't seem to be much of a difference in the first year or two of investing. However, over time, compound interest is a clear winner. Let's say you want to invest $10,000. Over 25 years, with an 8% return, a $10,000 investment can grow to $68,485 with compound interest! Simple interest with an 8% return only grows your investment to $20,000.

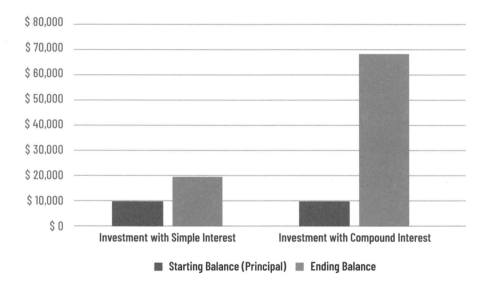

Compound interest helps investors earn more money than simple interest.

Remember that compound interest is calculated by paying interest on the principal (the amount of money you start with) and all the interest you earned from the past. Simple interest only applies to the principal.

Ending balance with compound interest = P × (1 + i)^n

Ending balance with simple interest = P × (1 + i × n)

P = Principal (the amount you're starting with)

i = Interest rate

n = Term (how many years you're saving)

1 = Principal plus interest

Simple interest can be more helpful if you borrow money. That's because as you make your payments, the interest payments will get lower over time. Many car loans work this way. However, compound interest will always be better when you invest money. Retirement accounts use compound interest to help people earn enough money to live off of during retirement.

Let's see interest in action! Calculate how much each investment below will be worth with compound interest and simple interest. You can also use an online interest calculator if you need help with the math. There is one in the Resources section on page 88. Check the answer key when you're finished.

PRINCIPAL	INTEREST RATE	TERM	ENDING BALANCE WITH SIMPLE INTEREST	ENDING BALANCE WITH COMPOUND INTEREST
$5,000	10% or 0.10	30 years		
$10,000	12% or 0.12	20 years		
$20,000	8% or 0.08	15 years		

MOTIVATIONAL MINDSET

If you are saving up for something big, it may take weeks or months before you have enough money. Waiting that long to buy something can feel like torture!

A trick to stick to your savings goal is to make it motivational. Read the list below of ways to stay motivated, and check off the ones that sound like fun to complete. Then, circle your favorite way and use it with your current savings goal.

☐ Draw boxes on a sheet of paper. Color in a box each time you deposit money into your savings account until you make your goal.

☐ Cut out a picture of your goal and hang it in a place where you can see it every day.

☐ Write three sentences on separate pieces of paper to motivate you to keep saving. Tape your motivational statements in different places around your home.

☐ Use a whiteboard to write your goal amount and how much you currently have saved. Write a new idea each week of how you will earn money toward your goal.

☐ Grab a sheet of paper and set a timer for three minutes. Without stopping until the timer ends, write down all of the reasons you want to save for your goal. Refer back to this list when you're feeling discouraged.

COLLEGE-BOUND

College is an exciting time for many students, but it is expensive to attend. A lot of students need student loans to pay for their education. If you are still in elementary school, you have something college students don't have—time!

You can start saving for college now through an investment account called a 529 plan. Money in a 529 plan can be used tax-free to pay for some education expenses, such as books and classes. A 529 plan often grows your money faster than a regular savings account because the money is invested in the stock market. The earlier you start, the more money you're likely to grow! Research a 529 plan with an adult's help and fill in the blanks below.

The name of the 529 plan for my state is:

_____

Do an online search for "What counts as a qualified 529 expense?"

What types of expenses qualify? _____

_____

_____

_____

BEST BANK

Unlike keeping money in a sock drawer at home, a bank will pay you to keep money in a savings account. Banks borrow money from people like you and lend it out to other customers. Then they pay you back with interest. Although the interest won't grow enough money for retirement, it's an easy way to grow your money for things, like a new scooter, without any extra work.

Be aware that banks have different interest rates and minimum account balances for savings accounts. Some also charge fees for things like taking more money from your account than you have. This is called an "overdraft fee." With an adult's help, research three banks either online or in person and fill in the table. Then decide which bank has the best savings account option.

	BANK 1	BANK 2	BANK 3
Monthly maintenance fee			
Overdraft fee			
Minimum account balance			
Interest rate			

Which bank has the best account? _____

ACCOUNTS WITH AN ADVANTAGE

There are two major types of accounts that you can open with a bank: checking and savings. A checking account is best for everyday spending. You can spend as much as you want from this account without paying any fees. However, most checking accounts earn very little to no interest. A savings account is best for saving money. Interest rates are higher, but there are limits on how often you can withdraw money each month.

Many people use checking accounts to pay their monthly bills. Savings accounts may be used for long-term savings goals, like buying a surfboard. Can you think of how you might use a checking and a savings account differently? Fill in the blanks below with your ideas.

I could use a checking account to pay for things like:

_____

_____

_____

I could use a savings account to save for things like:

_____

_____

_____

RETIREMENT RULES

When adults turn 59½ years old, they can start taking money from their retirement accounts without paying a penalty. Most people retire around this time (some retire even earlier!) and need income to pay for their living expenses well into their old age. This is why it's important to build up a large retirement account.

Many working adults use different retirement accounts such as a 401(k) or an individual retirement account (IRA). Retirement accounts have certain rules that investors must follow. Many have a contribution limit, meaning there is a limit to how much you can invest in a year. Ask an adult about their retirement plan using the questions below.

What type of retirement plan do you have?

_____

_____

What do you like best about your retirement plan?

_____

_____

What is one rule that you have to follow with your retirement

plan? _____

_____

_____

SAVVY SAVER

A savings account has all sorts of benefits. Firstly, it can help you save for small things like a new backpack. Secondly, a savings account can help you pay for big things like college or a house when you're older. Many people save money in this type of account for emergencies, too. Imagine needing money right away to replace a broken phone. A savings account lets you withdraw money easily for emergencies.

Be aware that there are limitations and rules you must follow with a savings account. For example, a savings account is not a good place to save for retirement because your money doesn't earn as much as it would in the stock market. You might also need to have a minimum account balance to avoid bank fees. How much do you know about savings accounts? Test your knowledge with the quiz below. Circle the correct answer for each question. If you're unsure on any of the answers, ask an adult for help. The answers are in the answer key.

1. **You can withdraw money from a savings account through an ATM or at a bank.**
   A. True
   B. False

2. **A savings account allows you to withdraw money as many times as you want.**
   A. True
   B. False

3. **A savings account typically . . .**
   A. pays interest.
   B. charges interest.
   C. has no interest.

4. **When you deposit money in a savings account, you are letting the bank borrow your money.**
   A. True
   B. False

LIST THE LOANS

A loan is money that is borrowed from a lender (a bank, credit union, or even a family member or friend) that must be repaid. Most loans that come from banks or other financial institutions are repaid with interest and within a certain period of time. Usually, the bigger the loan amount, the more time you have to pay it back.

There are several types of loans, including car loans, home loans, and personal loans. The interest rate and term—the amount of time you have to repay the loan—varies depending on the loan. Ask an adult to help you research different types of loans online. Then write down what you find in the spaces below.

	CAR LOAN	HOME LOAN/MORTGAGE	PERSONAL LOAN
Lender			
Interest rate			
Repayment term			

Which loan has the highest interest rate? _____

Which loan has the longest repayment term? _____

SORTING OUT SAVINGS

Banks offer three different kinds of savings accounts:

Traditional savings: pays a small amount of interest and you can take out money anytime.

Money market: pays more interest, but you must keep a larger amount of money in it.

Certificate of deposit (CD): pays more interest but you cannot take out money for a certain period of time.

Read about each person below and write on the line which account they need. Check your answers in the answer key.

1. Mark has $10,000. He wants to be able to use it for emergencies and earn interest. Mark needs this account:

   _____

2. Carlos has $3,000 that he wants to keep safe for twelve months. He wants to earn interest and doesn't need the cash right now. Carlos needs this account:

   _____

3. Deja has short- and long-term savings goals. She needs to be able to take money out often. Deja needs this account:

   _____

INTENTIONAL SAVER

There are several types of accounts that you can use to save and grow money. The account that is best for you will depend on your savings goal.

Savings account: a bank account that helps you save for short-term and long-term goals and earn interest.

Checking account: a bank account that lets you pay for everyday purchases.

Retirement account: an investment account that uses compound interest to grow money for retirement.

529 plan: an investment account to pay for some education expenses.

It's a good idea to have a blend of all types of accounts to help you save for your goals throughout your life. Write all of the money goals you have on the lines below. They can be short-term or long-term goals. You should have both! Then fill in the table on the following page to place your goals into the right type of account and assign a date by which you want to start saving for them.

My money goals: _____

_____

_____

_____

_____

_____

MY MONEY GOAL	WHEN I WANT TO START MY GOAL	WHAT TYPE OF ACCOUNT I NEED

ARE YOU A MONEY MASTER?

In this section, you learned about interest, bank accounts, and how to grow money. When you learn the basics of how to save and grow money when you are young, you're more likely to have healthy money habits later in life.

Can you think of an adult you know who has good money habits? Chances are they know how to grow their money and are a responsible saver. They may have even learned these skills early in life to become a money master. Now it's your turn! Test your money mastery by answering the following questions. If you don't know an answer, go back through the activities in this section to give you clues. Check your answers in the answer key.

1. **What is the major difference between simple and compound interest?**
   A. the way the interest is calculated
   B. the way the principal is calculated
   C. there is no difference

2. **What is a checking account mostly used for?**
   A. saving money
   B. spending on everyday purchases
   C. investing money

3. **When money is invested, what type of interest helps money grow the fastest?**
   A. compound interest
   B. simple interest
   C. complex interest

4. **When we talk about borrowing, saving, and growing money, what does principal mean?**
   A. the amount of money that is charged
   B. the amount of money you end with
   C. the amount of money you start with

STOCK MARKET SMARTY

Before you make your first investment, you need to know what to invest in. Investing can be scary because there are a lot of investing words to know. Luckily for you, you have this book with a quick reference guide! As you grow into an expert investor, you will come across these common investing terms:

Stock: a small piece of ownership in a company

Index: a measurement of how a group of investments performs

Index fund: a collection of stocks that track a specific index (i.e., S&P 500, Dow Jones)

Bond: a loan from an investor (like you) to a borrower that is paid back to the investor with interest

Mutual fund: a collection of investments, including stocks and bonds, made of money from many investors

Exchange-traded fund (ETF): a group of investments that can be traded like a stock

Cryptocurrency: digital or virtual currency that doesn't need a central bank or government to support it

As you start investing your money, you'll want to select investments that you feel confident about. That starts with some research! With an adult's help, research two or three companies that offer each type of investment and write what you find in the spaces on the following page. Then circle one company from each category that sounds interesting to you. Keep it in mind when you make your first investment!

STOCKS	INDEX FUNDS	INDEX

MUTUAL FUNDS	EXCHANGE-TRADED FUND (ETF)	CRYPTOCURRENCY	BONDS

GREAT RATES

Smart investors use a rate of return to measure whether they earned or lost money in an investment over time. Rates of return can be used for stocks, bonds, real estate, or even business growth. A positive rate of return means your investment is growing and earning money—nice work! A negative rate of return means your investment lost money.

Here is how to calculate the rate of return:

$$\textit{Rate of return} = \frac{\textit{End value} - \textit{Beginning value}}{\textit{Beginning value}} \times 100$$

Take a look at the beginning and end values of the stocks and bonds below. Calculate the rate of return for each.

	BEGINNING VALUE	END VALUE	RATE OF RETURN (WRITE OUT AS A PERCENTAGE)
Stock #1	$400	$600	
Stock #2	$25	$15	
Bond #1	$50	$65	
Bond #2	$100	$105	

1. Which investment had the best rate of return? _____

2. Which investment lost money? _____

3. Do you want investments that make money or lose money?

   _____

A LESSON IN LIQUIDITY

"Liquidity" is a term you'll come across when you manage money later in life. Liquidity is how quickly and easily you can get your hands on cash. Being able to get cash fast is helpful during an emergency. It's also helpful when you want to buy something right away.

Some cash is not needed until later, such as money you might be saving for retirement or other long-term investments. How liquid, or easy to get to, are each of the following accounts? Put each account under the correct column below. Then check the categories in the answer key.

- savings account
- 401(k) plan
- 529 college savings plan
- checking account
- piggy bank at home

MORE LIQUID	LESS LIQUID

ARE YOU A RISK-TAKER?

Life is full of risk. Think about riding a bike. When you ride down a steep hill, it's more exciting, but there's also a higher chance you could crash. If you take a flat path, it's much safer, but it's not as thrilling.

Investing is the same way. You could lose more money with a riskier investment. But you have a higher chance of earning money, too. What kind of risk-taker are you? For each scenario below, circle the letter next to the response that best describes you. Which letter did you circle most? Find the risk-taker type with that letter on the following page.

1. **When it comes to trying new food, I . . .**
   - **A.** immediately take a bite.
   - **B.** wait until someone else tries it first.
   - **C.** don't try it at all.

2. **When a new kid joins my class, I . . .**
   - **A.** introduce myself as soon as I can.
   - **B.** bring a friend and say hi.
   - **C.** avoid talking to them.

3. **When I go to the pool, I . . .**
   - **A.** jump off the high diving board.
   - **B.** go down the waterslide.
   - **C.** stay where I can touch the bottom.

Mostly As: Risk-seeker

You like high risks because the rewards are also high! Be sure to look at safer investments, like bonds, to balance out possible losses.

Mostly Bs: Risk-reviewer

You're comfortable with some risk, but you like safety measures, too. A blend of risky and safe investments will work best for you.

Mostly Cs: Risk-avoider

You want to know what to expect and like to feel safe. Consider some riskier investments, like stocks, so you don't miss out on possible big growth.

TAKING STOCK

Did you know that you can own part of a company? When you buy a company's stock, you are buying a piece (or share) of that company. In return, that company uses money from stocks to run their business and, hopefully, create a profit for everyone. Stocks are bought and sold on stock exchanges like the New York Stock Exchange (NYSE) or NASDAQ.

Stock exchanges use ticker symbols to easily identify each company. A ticker symbol stands for the company's name. Apple's ticker symbol is AAPL, for example. Let's take a look at a few companies you can buy stock from. With an adult's help, look up the ticker symbol of each company in the table below. Write down how much the stock costs. Then circle which one you would invest in.

COMPANY	TICKER SYMBOL	STOCK PRICE
Coca-Cola Co.		
Ford Motor Company		
Walt Disney Co.		

DIVIDEND DETECTIVE

There are two ways you can make money from stocks. The first is to sell your stock for a higher price than you paid for it. The second way is from dividends. A dividend is a payment to the stockholder (you) from the company's profits.

To figure out how much of a dividend a stock pays, you'll need to take the dividend yield (usually listed as a percentage) and divide it by 100. Then multiply it by the price per share (of stock):

Dividend amount = (Dividend yield ÷ 100) x Price per share

Using the information you found for the *Taking Stock* activity on page 66, go back online with an adult and record the dividend yield (if any) for each stock. Then figure out the dividend amount for each.

COMPANY	DIVIDEND YIELD	DIVIDEND AMOUNT
Coca-Cola Co.		
Ford Motor Company		
Walt Disney Co.		

CRYPTOCURRENCY: COMPLICATED OR CLEVER?

You know about paper bills, coins, and credit cards, but did you know there is a new currency in the world? Cryptocurrency is a computer-based replacement for physical money. Cryptocurrency is not controlled by a central bank or government, so you don't need to open a bank account for it. All you need is internet access! People all around the world can use the same cryptocurrency, which means there are no exchange rates for it.

Cryptocurrency is pretty new, which makes it unpredictable. No one knows how much value it will gain or lose over time, and many businesses don't accept it as a form of payment. Cryptocurrency also requires a lot of computing power, which requires a lot of electricity.

Do you think cryptocurrency is better than our current money system? Why or why not?

_____

_____

_____

_____

_____

_____

_____

INTENTIONAL INVESTMENTS

There are many ways to invest your money, including individual stocks or real estate (buying houses or stores). You can even invest in things people collect such as playing cards. Did you know that in the 1990s, people invested in plush toys called Beanie Babies? People thought they'd be worth thousands of dollars today, but many sell for just a few dollars. Beanie Babies weren't a good investment!

Below is a list of things you can invest in. Check the box next to each investment type that sounds interesting to you. Which investment do you think would make you the most money? Discuss your favorite type of investment with an adult.

☐ Stocks

☐ Sports playing cards

☐ Bonds

☐ Art

☐ Real estate (houses or retail shops)

☐ Cryptocurrency

☐ Collectible toys

☐ Index funds

☐ Mutual funds

☐ Classic video games

FINANCIALLY FEARLESS

Have you ever lost money? How did you feel about it? You might have felt anxious or angry. People can feel that way when they lose money in the stock market. When an investment isn't performing well, some people get scared and sell it so that they don't lose even more money.

However, those who wait to sell until an investment goes back up get rewarded. It can be hard to be patient, though! Remember that you don't lose money in an investment until you sell it at a lower price than you bought it. Investing can make you feel all kinds of emotions, from really excited to very anxious.

Describe which emotion you would feel for each of these scenarios.

You have $500 invested in the stock market and it loses $50 of its

value in one day. _____

You make a monthly contribution of $20 in the stock market.

_____

You open your very first investment account.

_____

You lose $100 in value in the stock market in one day. Three weeks later, your investment is worth $500 more.

_____

A ROLLER COASTER OF RISK

These days, buying stock is as simple as tapping a button on your phone. It is easy to purchase stock—and it can be just as easy to lose or earn money. Investing in stocks is like riding a roller coaster. You have to brace yourself for any scary drops that might come your way!

Let's take a look at PepsiCo, maker of Lay's potato chips, Pepsi soda, and other tasty snacks and drinks. Go online with an adult and record how much the price of one share of PepsiCo (PEP) has either increased or decreased for each time period listed below.

TIME PERIOD	INCREASE OR DECREASE IN PRICE PER SHARE
Past week	
Past month	
Past three months	
Past year	
Past five years	

Which time period(s) had a decrease in price per share?

_____

Which time period had the highest increase in price per share?

_____

PLAYING IT SAFE

Although stock investments are like a roller coaster, low-risk, low-reward investments like certificates of deposit (CDs) are more of a bike ride in the park. You are guaranteed that you will make money on your investment. It will just be a much smaller amount.

A CD is a way to loan your money to a bank for a certain length of time. In exchange, the bank will pay you back with interest. The catch is that you can't touch that money until it reaches maturity (the date you can take your money out).

With an adult's help, research three CDs at three different banks and fill in the table below with the minimum amount to open the CD, maturity date, and the annual percentage yield (interest rate). Then circle the best option.

BANK	MINIMUM AMOUNT TO OPEN	MATURITY DATE	ANNUAL PERCENTAGE YIELD (APY)

RISK AND REWARD

As we've discussed, investing money has a certain level of risk. Usually the higher the risk, the higher the reward. The lower the risk, the lower the reward. Remember that savings accounts usually pay only a small amount of interest. There's no risk of losing your money with a savings account, but don't expect to gain a lot of money, either.

If you were to invest in stocks on the stock market, you have a higher chance of earning a profit, but a greater chance of losing money. This balance between risk and reward is called the "risk/reward trade-off."

Investing is a balance between risk and reward.

Take a look at the following investment types. Draw either an up arrow or a down arrow next to each to indicate whether the investment is low-risk or high-risk. Check the answer key to see if you got it right.

_____ **Stocks**

_____ **Savings accounts**

_____ **Bonds**

_____ **Cryptocurrency**

SPEND OR INVEST?

It's fun to buy new stuff, like the latest phone or sneakers, but have you ever thought about buying stock in the companies that make the phone and the sneakers? There is a major difference between buying goods and buying stock: appreciation and depreciation.

Appreciation: going up in value; an increase in worth.

Depreciation: going down in value; a decrease in worth.

Usually, goods depreciate and stocks appreciate. Suppose you could buy either a popular product or the company stock. Thinking about appreciation and depreciation, which would you choose? Take a look at the examples below and circle which ones you would buy.

iPhone or Apple stock

Nike Air sneakers or Nike stock

Mickey Mouse backpack or Disney stock

Now look at the following page to see how the price of the products and company stocks changed with time.

	VALUE IN 2010	VALUE IN 2021
iPhone 4	$199	$70
Apple stock	$7.57 per share	$179.45 per share
2010 Nike Air shoes	$100	$45
Nike stock	$15.94 per share	$166.67 per share
Mickey Mouse backpack	$25	$50
Disney stock	$32.75 per share	$157.07 per share

Now, would you rather buy the products or the stocks?

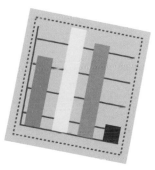

HOUSE GOALS

Did you know that buying a home is actually an investment? Home ownership is an example of a physical asset (something of value) that appreciates (increases in value) over time. As with any investment, you'll need to do a lot of research in order to make money and avoid losing money. Before purchasing a home, the buyer needs to know a few terms:

Down payment: cash that a buyer puts toward the purchase of a home.

Mortgage: a loan used to purchase a home. It is usually the home price minus the down payment.

Mortgage interest rate: the interest for the mortgage that the borrower must pay.

Equity: the amount of money you keep when you sell a home. It is how much the home is worth minus the mortgage amount.

A down payment decreases the amount of money you need to borrow. The bigger the down payment, the smaller your monthly mortgage payment. Many people use 20% of the house cost as a down payment. For example, if you want to buy a house that costs $200,000, you'd pay $40,000 (20%) as a down payment. This is a lot of money for most people. That's why it's important to save often and early! Read the example on the following page and write in your answers. Check the answer key when you're finished.

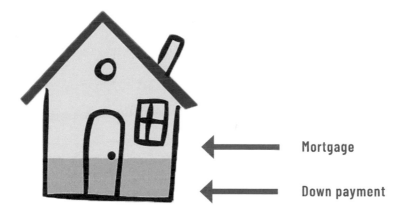

Mortgage

Down payment

Home price: $400,000
Interest rate: 4% or 0.04

1. How much do you need for a down payment (home price x 20% or 0.20)? _____

2. How much will you need to borrow through a mortgage?

    _____

3. How much will you pay in interest for the year (interest rate x mortgage amount)?

    _____

4. If the value of your home increases to $450,000, how much equity will you have?

    _____

CAR COSTS

You just learned that houses are good investments. What about another expensive item—cars? In most cases, cars go down in value after they are purchased. Rare and classic cars that are in perfect condition are exceptions.

New cars bought from dealerships tend to depreciate the most. According to Experian, new cars lose 20% of their value within the first year of ownership and 10% every year afterward. That means in five years, your new car could be worth 50% less than what you bought it for. Imagine buying a $70,000 sports car and finding it's worth only $35,000 five years later. Losing $35,000 is not a very good investment!

Calculate how much a brand-new SUV is worth each year after it's purchased using the price tag figure below. Then check your answers in the answer key.

BRAND-NEW SUV	PRICE TAG: $67,000
Year 1	
Year 2	
Year 3	
Year 4	
Year 5	

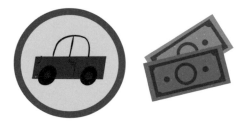

BUILDING WITH BONDS

A bond is a loan from an investor to a borrower that is paid back to the investor with interest. Like CDs, they are a low-risk, low-reward investment. Companies and governments offer bonds as a way to raise money to pay for various projects, such as building schools or researching the development of a new product. Answer the question about bonds below, then check your answer in the answer key.

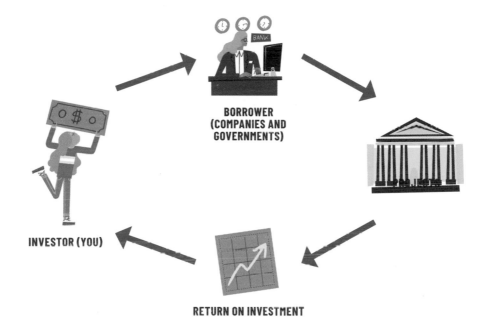

BORROWER
(COMPANIES AND
GOVERNMENTS)

INVESTOR (YOU)

RETURN ON INVESTMENT

Your local government wants to repair several highways and make a new bridge in town. They need money for the project, so they create a bond to sell to the public. They promise to pay investors 5% or 0.05 in interest on the bond.

If you invest \$1,000 in these government bonds, how much money will you receive in interest in one year? _____

FUN WITH INDEX FUNDS

An index fund is a collection of stocks that follows the growth and losses of a specific stock market index, like the S&P 500. When you buy an index fund, you buy a little piece of every company listed in that index. This is usually lower risk than buying a single stock.

When you invest in hundreds of companies in one index fund, you don't have to worry about a single stock doing poorly. Go online with an adult's help and look up an index fund. Fill out the index fund profile below.

Index fund name: _____

Index fund ticker symbol: _____

What are some companies the index fund invests in?

_____

_____

_____

Is the index fund high- or low-risk? _____

What is the rate of return? _____

Would you invest in this fund? Why or why not?

_____

_____

_____

EGGCELLENT INVESTMENTS

Have you ever heard the saying, "Don't put all of your eggs in one basket"? It's good advice. If that one basket breaks or topples over, all your eggs are ruined. It's better to put your eggs in several baskets. This advice goes for investing, too. You should put your money in several investments (or baskets). That way, if one of your investment baskets loses money, you still have some money safe in other baskets (funds) to fall back on. This is called "diversification."

Index funds　　　**Stocks**　　　**Bonds**

How would you diversify your investments? Color in how many Investment eggs you would put into each basket. Remember which are high-risk and low-risk investments so you can decide how many eggs you'd like to put there.

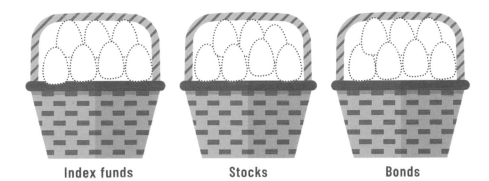

Index funds　　　**Stocks**　　　**Bonds**

TEST YOUR INVESTOR SKILLS

Investing isn't that complicated. You have worked through real-life examples of investing throughout this activity book and are more prepared than some adults!

Ready to put your investor skills to the test? Take the mini quiz below by circling the correct answer for each question. Check the answer key to see how you did.

1. **Which type of account is more liquid?**
   - **A.** 401(k) retirement plan
   - **B.** savings account

2. **What abbreviation do you use when you want to look up a company in the stock market?**
   - **A.** stock symbol
   - **B.** finance symbol
   - **C.** ticker symbol

3. **What is a dividend?**
   - **A.** a payment to the stockholder from the company's profits
   - **B.** a charge on top of a loan that you have to pay back
   - **C.** a fee you have to pay to invest in the stock market

4. **How risky is it to invest in a bond?**
   - **A.** high risk
   - **B.** no risk
   - **C.** low risk

5. **Which of these is true about compound interest?**
   - **A.** It is paid on the principal (money you start with) plus all past earned interest.
   - **B.** It helps grow investments over time.
   - **C.** It helps investors earn more money than simple interest.
   - **D.** All of the above.

DARE TO DREAM

One of the biggest reasons people invest is to be able to retire and stop working when they are older. Imagine all of the things you could do if you had enough money saved for retirement. Many people dream about the things they'd like to do after they retire. Now it's your turn.

Take a look at the ideas below. Check the box next to each activity that you would like to do when you have enough money in your investment accounts to retire. Fill in your own ideas in the blank spaces.

☐ Travel around the world

☐ Spend time with family

☐ Build a house you design

☐ Buy a sports car

☐ Go fishing

☐ Visit all of the national parks

☐ Spend time with friends

☐ Go to the beach

☐ Try a new hobby

☐ Take an art class

☐ Play video games

☐ Read books

☐ Buy a pool

☐ Learn how to bake

☐ Get a new pet

☐ Write a book

☐ _____

☐ _____

☐ _____

Answer Key

Making Money

Mowing for Money: 1. 5 lawns; 2. $20 per lawn

Tax Time: 1. $100; 2. $50; 3. $850 ($1,000 - $150)

Payment and Cash Categories: Types of Money: $10 bill, $1 bill, quarter, dime, $20 bill; Types of Payment: check, credit card, money order, app, debit card

That's How the Cookie Crumbles: 1. $20; 2. $0.40; 3. $30

Responsible Spending

Expense Explorer: Fixed Expenses: lunch money, groceries, electricity, transportation; Variable Expenses: phone app, jeans, pencils, movie tickets, beach vacation

Budget-Buster: 1. -$75; 2. over budget; 3. eliminate concerts or the vacation fund, or reduce groceries or clothing

Creating a Credit Score: Things that improve a credit score: paying bills on time, paying the electric bill each month, spending money on things you can afford, paying your credit card bill each month, paying off student loans

Interest in Action: 1. $6.16; 2. $9.04; 3. $12.33

Debit vs. Credit: Debit: groceries, new computer, electricity bill; Credit: paycheck, interest

The Savings Equation: video game console: 8 months; ticket to Disney World: $12.50 per month; art supply set: 2 months; headphones: $40 per month

Saving and Growing Money

Now or Later?:

WEEKS	NICHOLAS NOW		LUCY LATER	
	SPENT	TOTAL SAVED	SPENT	TOTAL SAVED
WEEK 1	$5	$0	$1	$4
WEEK 2	$5	$0	$1	$8
WEEK 3	$0	$5	$1	$12
WEEK 4	$0	$10	$1	$16
WEEK 5	$0	$15	$1	$20
WEEK 6	$0	$20		

Nicholas Now has to wait six weeks to purchase the game and doesn't buy candy for four weeks. Lucy Later waits only five weeks to purchase the game and gets candy each week.

Simple Cents: $3,000; $28,000

Goal-Getter: Answers may vary depending on how much the item costs. Short-term: candy, colored pencil set, board game, book, puzzle, basketball; long-term: sneakers, headphones, video game console, phone

Compound Interest: $10,469

Simple vs. Compound Interest:

PRINCIPAL	INTEREST RATE	TERM	ENDING BALANCE WITH SIMPLE INTEREST	ENDING BALANCE WITH COMPOUND INTEREST
$5,000	10% or 0.10	30 years	$20,000	$87,247
$10,000	12% or 0.12	20 years	$34,000	$96,463
$20,000	8% or 0.08	15 years	$44,000	$63,443

Savvy Saver: 1. a; 2. b; 3. a; 4. a

Sorting Out Savings: 1. money market; 2. CD; 3. traditional savings

Are You a Money Master?: 1. a; 2. b; 3. a; 4. c

Investing Money

Great Rates: Stock #1: 50%; Stock #2: -40%; Bond #1: 30%; Bond #2: 5%; 1. Stock #1; 2. Stock #2; 3. make money

A Lesson in Liquidity: More Liquid: savings account, checking account, piggy bank at home; Less Liquid: 401(k) plan, 529 college savings plan

Taking Stock: Coca-Cola Co. (KO), Ford Motor Company (F), Walt Disney Co. (DIS); Stock prices will vary.

Risk and Reward: Stocks: ↑; Savings accounts: ↓; Bonds: ↓; Cryptocurrency: ↑

House Goals: 1. $80,000; 2. $320,000; 3. $12,800; 4. $130,000

Car Costs: Year 1: $53,600; Year 2: $48,240; Year 3: $43,416; Year 4: $39,074.40; Year 5: $35,166.96

Building with Bonds: $50

Test Your Investor Skills: 1. b; 2. c; 3. a; 4. c; 5. d

Resources

Books

Andal, Walter. **Finance 101 for Kids: Money Lessons Children Cannot Afford to Miss**. Grove City, Ohio: Gatekeeper Press, 2016. This book makes learning about saving and investing fun!

My First Step in Crypto and Bitcoin Investing for Kids and Beginners. Sweet Smart Books, 2021.
Is cryptocurrency something that interests you? This book is a great introduction.

Redling, Dylin and Allison Tom. **Investing for Kids: How to Save, Invest, and Grow Money**. Emeryville, CA: Rockridge Press, 2020. This book is the companion to this activity book. Learn about different types of investments and how to grow your money.

What Are Stocks?: Understanding the Stock Market. Newark, DE: Baby Professor, 2017.
Stocks can be confusing, but this book helps answer all your questions about investing in the stock market.

Websites

BizKids.com
Thinking of starting a business? Get motivated and learn from kids that have done just that! This site also features lots of fun videos that explain financial topics.

Easy Peasy Finance YouTube Channel

YouTube.com/easypeasyfinance
   Learn investing concepts in quick and entertaining videos with twelve-year-old Rishi Vamdatt:

MarketWatch.com
   Look up information on specific stocks, bonds, and read up on financial and business news.

Online Compound Interest Calculator

Investor.gov/financial-tools-calculators/calculators/compound -interest-calculator
   This calculator will make figuring out compound interest much easier.

TheMint.org
   Features fun quizzes, calculators, and suggestions for earning, saving, spending, and giving money. Just click on the tab titled "fun for kids."

Acknowledgments

And the World's Best Supporting Husband Award goes to . . . Kyle Nelson! Thank you for picking up the parenting slack while I put my whole heart into this book. My sincere appreciation to Ellie Kay who gave me the confidence to say yes to this project and consider me an author. Lastly, thank you to LAKEY INSPIRED and every song that he has ever produced. Listening to those songs on repeat created an inspiring writing environment that kept my ideas flowing.

About the Author

 **JUSTINE NELSON** is the face and founder of Debt Free Millennials, a website and YouTube channel aimed at helping overwhelmed millennials improve their money situation without giving up the avocado toast. Justine was named a "YouTuber to Watch" in *Forbes* for her simple, actionable financial tips, exploring debt, saving, and budgeting. She paid off $35,000 in student loan debt in two and a half years on a $37,000 salary. Now she's teaching other millennials how to crush debt and live payment-free. When she's not in front of the camera, Justine loves exploring San Diego with her husband and baby girl.